Guide to Out-of-Print Materials

Narda Tafuri
Anna Seaberg
Gary Handman

Acquisitions Guides, No. 12

Association for Library Collections & Technical Services,
A Division of the American Library Association
Published in cooperation with
The Scarecrow Press, Inc., Lanham, Maryland
2004

SCARECROW PRESS, INC.

Published in the United States of America
by Scarecrow Press, Inc.
A wholly owned subsidiary of
The Rowman & Littlefield Publishing Group, Inc.
4501 Forbes Boulevard, Suite 200, Lanham, Maryland 20706
www.scarecrowpress.com

PO Box 317
Oxford
OX2 9RU, UK

British Library Cataloguing in Publication Information Available

Library of Congress Cataloging-in-Publication Data

Tafuri, Narda, 1954–
   Guide to out-of-print materials / Narda Tafuri, Anna Seaberg, Gary Handman.
     p. cm. — (Acquisitions guides ; no. 12)
   Includes bibliographical references.
   ISBN 0-8108-4974-7 (pbk. : alk. paper)
  1. Libraries—Special collections—Out-of-print materials. 2. Out-of-print
materials—Purchasing. I. Seaberg, Anna, 1956– II. Handman, Gary, 1950–
III. Title. IV. Series.
Z689 .A2746 1973 no. 12 [Z692.O95]
025.21—dc22   2003019656

Contents

Part I

Introduction

1. Role of Out-of-Print Materials

1.1 Purpose of the Guide

The purpose of this guide is to provide an overview of both the traditional and online resources available to the acquisitions librarian in locating and acquiring materials that are considered to be out of print. It is meant to assist, direct, and instruct librarians in locating and purchasing out-of-print materials. It is by no means a comprehensive guide providing all resources that may be available.

The acquisition of out-of-print materials is not always straightforward. It may be necessary to use a combination of techniques, traditional and online, to achieve the best results. Acquisitions librarians may also be restricted in the types of techniques they are able to use by the regulations of the institutions in which they are employed.

Finally, we should note here that even though the Internet has made out-of-print materials more accessible, not every out-of-print item is available for purchase. Each librarian must decide for him- or herself how long to pursue an individual item.

1.2 Organization of the Guide

The acquisition of out-of-print materials provides unique challenges to the acquisitions librarian. The techniques for locating and purchasing an item are specific to the type of item being acquired. Therefore, the system of resources available for the acquisition of out-of-print books is not the same as that available for out-of-print audiovisual materials or serials.

This guide is organized in separate sections based on the type of material being acquired, books, audiovisual materials, and serials, and includes an opening section providing general information.

1.3 Need for Out-of-Print Materials in Libraries

The need for out-of-print materials exists the moment a library requests that a book, magazine, video, etc. be acquired and the publisher declares that item to be "out of print." It is currently estimated that the average book will become out of print within 18 months of its initial publication.

Other situations requiring the purchase of out-of-print materials may include, but are not limited to, the replacement of materials that are still needed but have been determined by the library to be missing, incomplete, or irreparable.

1.4 Distinguishing Antiquarian, Rare, and Out-of-Print Materials

There are many terms used to describe what are generally thought of as "out-of-print" books. An out-of-print title can be described by any or all of the following terms. These terms and their descriptions are those generally agreed upon by most booksellers.

1.4.1 Antiquarian
   Antiquarian refers to the age of a book, serial, or other material. An item that is from the nineteenth century or earlier is generally considered to be antiquarian. However, the age of an item does not indicate its rarity or out-of-print status.
1.4.2 Rare
   An item that is rare is one that has had a very limited distribution and/or of which very few complete copies remain. Rare items are not usually readily available for purchase. A rare item can be one-of-a-kind with no other copies existing. The rarity of an item may affect its price.
1.4.3 Out-of-Print (OP)
   An item is considered out of print when a publisher has declared it to be so. This means that the publisher has relin-

quished the rights to publish the item and, depending on the contract, the rights may have reverted to the author. An item that a publisher considers "out of stock indefinitely" often becomes out of print sometime in the near future. Some additional terms relating to out-of-print materials include:

1.4.4　Out of Stock Indefinitely (OSI)

An item becomes out of stock indefinitely when the publisher still maintains the publishing rights but has no immediate plans in the foreseeable future to reprint the item.

1.4.5　Secondhand

Items that are secondhand have been previously owned or are used, but may or may not be out of print. Many out-of-print dealers sell used books, though these books may still be available for purchase new from the publisher or at a substantially reduced price as used or secondhand copies.

1.4.6　Out-of-Distribution

Although audiovisual materials may still be covered under copyright laws, they may no longer be in distribution. In other words, copies are no longer available new from the original distributor. The only copies available in this case will be remaindered or used copies.

Part II

Guide for Acquiring Out-of-Print Materials

2. General Information

2.1 Traditional Means of Acquiring Out-of-Print Materials

Prior to the Internet, the acquisition of out-of-print materials was accomplished through posting lists of titles wanted in print publications, contacting dealers with specialties in subject areas, and maintaining paper lists of out-of-print titles. Serials were often acquired in microform.

Any or all of these methods can still be a valuable means of locating and acquiring out-of-print items.

2.1.1 Advantages to Using Traditional Means to Acquire Out-of-Print Materials

(a) Decrease in Use of Staff Time
Using the Internet to locate out-of-print items still requires a library staff member to spend time searching, inquiring about the availability and condition, and acquiring a needed item. For example, a knowledgeable subject-specialist out-of-print bookseller can often perform this task with better results.

(b) Expanded Access to All Out-of-Print Resources
Not all out-of-print dealers have their materials listed on the Internet. Of those dealers that do have out-of-print items listed online, most have only a small percentage of their total inventory available there. Posting lists of

wanted titles or contacting dealers with subject specialties would reach a larger number of dealers, thus in-
creasing the probability of locating the out-of-print materials you are looking for. An out-of-print book dealer
could also handle these tasks, similarly eliminating the
need for additional staff time.

2.1.2 Disadvantages to Using Traditional Means to Acquire Out-of-
Print Materials

    (a) Maintenance of Paper Lists
        Staff time is needed to prepare and accurately maintain
        lists of wanted items or to check lists of duplicates of-
        fered by other libraries.
    (b) Increased Cost of Items Purchased
        Items purchased through an out-of-print bookseller who
        acquires the items on your behalf will be more expensive
        than items ordered directly, since the bookseller will nor-
        mally put a surcharge on the item to cover his/her ex-
        penses plus a percentage for profit.

2.2 Acquiring Out-of-Print Materials in the Era of the Web

2.2.1 Searching for Out-of-Print Materials on Websites
The following points should be considered when using Internet sources to locate and acquire out-of-print materials.

    (a) Each out-of-print website has a slightly different search
        engine and way of indexing its materials. Unless a very
        specific copy of an item is required, it is best to try a min-
        imalistic search strategy, for example, by the author's last
        name and title keywords, to obtain the best search results.
        If possible, sort by price to locate least expensive copy.
    (b) Out-of-print websites are not always as up-to-date as one
        might expect. If a database shows a title as available, the
        dealer should be contacted before sending payment as of-
        ten a title may have previously been sold but not yet re-
        moved from the database.
    (c) Out-of-print dealers generally accept checks and credit
        cards. Some, but not all, will ship materials with an invoice.

(d) Prices of out-of-print materials on the Web do not generally conform to current print price guides. For example, a Web price for an out-of-print book can be very different than what is found in a print price guide that is based on auction sales and reported dealer sales.

(e) Just as in the print world, the world of cyberspace lends itself to a variety of scams, such as dealers selling non-existent merchandise or identity theft. Use the same caution as you would use when dealing with an unknown bookseller or publisher. Seek recommendations from colleagues or use third party services, such as Abebooks, Alibris, Blackwell's, or Midwest Library Service, to reduce risk.

(f) Internet companies are constantly changing, merging, or going out of business. Information about companies mentioned in this guide must be viewed as transitory.

3. Books

3.1 How to Locate Out-of-Print Dealers

3.1.1 Inclusive Print Directories
Many of the currently available print directories of out-of-print booksellers are quite old; however, they can still be useful. Some dealers listed in these directories may still be in business. (Book titles listed here are cited completely in the bibliography of this guide.)

- Local Telephone Directory Listings
- *Buy Books Where—Sell Books Where, 1994–1995* (Robinson 1994)
- *Antiquarian, Specialty, and Used Book Sellers: A Subject Guide and Directory, 1997–98* (Ethridge and Ethridge 1997)

3.1.2 Organizations
Antiquarian bookseller organizations often have lists of their members available by geographic location as well as subject specialties. Booksellers that are members of professional organizations generally must follow their organization's code of ethics.

(a) Local Bookseller Organizations—United States
     The following is a listing of some, but not all, of the local
     antiquarian booksellers organizations. Most have web-
     sites that include directories of their members as well as
     other information regarding their organizations.

1. Florida Antiquarian Booksellers Association (FABA)
   http://floridabooksellers.com
2. Georgia Antiquarian Booksellers Association (GABA)
   http://www.gaba.net
3. Long Island Antiquarian Book Dealers Association
   (LIABDA)
   http://liabda.com
   liabda@optonline.net; P.O. Box 42, Manhasset, NY
   11030
4. Maine Antiquarian Booksellers Association (MABA)
   http://www.mainebooksellers.org
   info@mainbooksellers.org
5. Massachusetts and Rhode Island Antiquarian Booksellers (MARIAB)
   http://www.mariab.org
6. Midwest Bookhunters
   http://www.midwestbookhunters.org
   1759 Rosehill Drive, Chicago, IL 60660; (773) 989-
   2200; (773) 989-7599 fax
7. New Hampshire Antiquarian Booksellers Association
   (NHABA)
   http://www.nhaba.org
8. Northern Ohio Bibliophilic Society (NOBS)
   http://www.csuohio.edu/CUT/nobs.htm
   Contact: Frank Klein, NOBS President, The Booksellers, Inc., 174 W. Exchange St., Akron, OH 44302;
   (330) 762-3101; j-fklein@msn.com
9. Rocky Mountain Antiquarian Booksellers Association
   (RMABA)
   http://www.rmaba.org
10. San Diego Booksellers Association (SDBA)
    http://www.keeline.com/SDBA/
    Contact: Gere McGilvery, Membership Coordinator,
    (619) 456-6623

11. Seattle Used Bookstore Guide
    http://recollectionbooks.com/seattle.html
12. Vermont Antiquarian Booksellers Association (VABA)
    http://www.valley.net/~vaba/
13. Washington Antiquarian Booksellers Association (WABA)
    http://www.wababooks.com

(b) Local Bookseller Organizations—Foreign
    The following is a partial listing of foreign bookseller organizations organized by country. Addresses are included if available.

1. Australia
   http://www.anzaab.com
   Australian and New Zealand Association of Antiquarian Booksellers Limited
   604 High Street, Prahan, Victoria, Australia
2. Belgium
   La Chambre professionnelle Belge de la Librarie Ancienne et Moderne
   http://www.clam-bba.be
3. Canada
   Antiquarian Booksellers' Association of Canada
   http://www.abac.org
   ABAC/ALAC, 4376 West 10th Ave., Vancouver, BC V6R 2H7 Canada
4. Denmark
   Danish Antiquarian Booksellers Association
   http://www.antikvar.dk
   Postboks 2028, DK-1210 Kobenhavn K Denmark; antikvar@vip.cybercity.dk
5. France
   Syndicat national de la Librairie Ancienne et Moderne
   http://www.slam-livre.fr
   4, rue Git-le-Coeur, 75006 Paris, France; (+33) 1 43 29 46 38; (+33) 1 43 25 41 63; slam@worldnet.fr
6. Germany
   Verband Deutscher Antiquare, E.V.
   http://www.antiquare.de/kern.html

7. Italy
   Associazione Librai Antiquari d'Italia (Antiquarian
   Booksellers Association of Italy)
   http://www.alai.it
   Via Jacopo Nardi 6-50132 Firenze, Italy; +39 (055) 243
   253 phone and fax; alai@alai.it
8. Netherlands
   Nederlandsche Vereeniging van Antiquaren (Dutch
   Antiquarian Booksellers' Association)
   http://www.nvva.nl
   Contact: Gert Jan Bestebreurtje, Secretary of NvVA,
   Postbus 364, 3400 AJ Utrecht, Netherlands; (030) 231
   92 86; (030) 234 33 62 fax; bestbook@wxs.nl
9. Sweden
   Svenska Antikvariatföreningen (Swedish Antiquarian
   Booksellers' Association)
   http://www.svaf.se
   Box 22549, SE-104 22 Stockholm, Sweden;
   main@svaf.se
10. Switzerland
    Association of Swiss Antiquarian Book and Print
    Dealers
    http://www.vebuku.ch
    vebuku info@sigrist.ch
11. United Kingdom
    Antiquarian Booksellers' Association
    http://www.aba.org.uk
    Sackville House, 40 Piccadilly, London W1J 0DR
    United Kingdom; +44 (020) 7439 3118; +44 (020) 7439
    3119 fax; info@aba.org.uk

(c) National and International Organizations

1. Antiquarian Booksellers' Association of America
   (ABAA)
   http://abaa.org
   20 West 44th Street, 4th floor, New York, NY 10036-
   6604; (212) 944-8291; (212) 944-8293 fax; inquiries@
   abaa.org

    2.   International League of Antiquarian Booksellers
        (ILAB)
        http://www.ilab-lila.com
        info@ilab-lila.com

3.1.3 Web Directories
(See section 3.2 and 3.3.2 for complete listing and contact information.)

  (a) Bookwire
  (b) AcqWeb
  (c) Advanced Book Exchange (Abebooks)
  (d) Alibris

3.1.4 Print Sources for Listing Active Wants
Many out-of-print dealers do not list their entire stock of books on the Internet. These dealers can be valuable sources of out-of-print materials.

One way of reaching these dealers is to list the titles of the books you are interested in purchasing in trade magazines and periodicals. The advent of the Internet has seen many of these publications disappear; however, the following remain vital resources for acquiring out-of-print materials.

  (a) *AB Bookman's Weekly: For the Specialist Book World* (discontinued)
    Published weekly. Jacob L. Chernofsky, editor.
    Called *Antiquarian Bookman* until 1967, this publication began in 1948 and folded in May 2000. *AB Bookman's Weekly* was one of the best-known out-of-print dealer trade publications. Classified ads, editorials, as well as informative articles dealing with the out-of-print and antiquarian book trade were included. Although no longer in publication, *AB Bookman's Weekly*, and the standards set by this publication, are often referred to by out-of-print booksellers.
  (b) *Bookdealer*
    Published weekly. Barry Shaw, editor.
    One of the leading British publications for the out-of-print and antiquarian book trade. Every issue contains many

thousands of titles wanted or for sale. Editorials and classified ads are included. There is a charge of 27 pence (approximately $.45) per line for books wanted and 24 pence for books for sale. Wants should be formatted as "author, title." Checks in U.S. currency are accepted. For additional information, contact: *Bookdealer*, Eastern Wing, Banwell Castle, Banwell, Weston-super-Mare BS29 6NX, United Kingdom; +44 (01934) 822 971; +44 (01934) 820 682 fax; alacrity@dial.pipex.com.

(c) *Firsts: The Book Collector's Magazine*
Published monthly. Kathryn Smiley, editor.
Firsts is a magazine for anyone who loves books and collects first edition books. Editorials, classified ads, and articles are included. Classified ads containing wants may be faxed, mailed, e-mailed, or phoned in. There is a flat rate of $1.00 per word for upper and lower case. For additional information contact: P.O. Box 65166, Tucson, AZ 85728-5166; (520) 529-1355; (520) 529-5847 fax; firsts-mag@aol.com; http://www.firsts.com.

(d) *OP Magazine: Book Culture, Collectors & Commerce*
Published bimonthly. Dee Stewart, editor.
True to its tagline, *OP Magazine* is focused on "book culture, collectors, and commerce." It contains articles dealing with the impact of technology, international trends, and new directions in book selling and collecting. *OP* is dedicated to the out-of-print, collectible, and antiquarian book world. Classified ads start at $15 for up to 30 words. For additional information contact: Dee Stewart, P.O. Box 3397, Santa Rosa, CA 95402; (707) 569-9257, phone and fax; info@opmagazine.com; http://www.opmagazine.com.

3.2 Directories and Indexes to Out-of-Print Resources on the Web

These sites provide copious Web sources for information on out-of-print books and materials and link to numerous out-of-print dealer and search sites.

3.2.1 *AcqWeb*: http://acqweb.library.vanderbilt.edu
Accessible through the link "Out-of-Print, Rare and Antiquar-

ian Agents" in the "Verification Tools and Resources" section of the AcqWeb home page's table of contents. Provides links to out-of-print search engines and associations that provide simultaneous searching of out-of-print vendor and bookseller databases. Listings include both North American and European vendors and booksellers. (See Section 3.3.3 for information ACQNET listserv.)

3.2.2 *Books and Book Collecting*: http://www.trussel.com/f_booksx .htm

Developed by Steve Trussel, this is the ultimate resource for book collectors, librarians, or anyone looking for either new or used books via the Web. Provides links to and searches of multiple out-of-print book databases. A one-stop source for online book resources. In addition, Trussel has created "Book-Seek," an index that is updated daily with catalog pages from used, rare, and out-of-print book dealers that are not searchable in any of the other out-of-print database sites.

3.2.3 *Bookwire*: http://www.bookwire.com/bookwire/booksellers/ antiquarian-booksellers.html

Bookwire has one of the largest selections of links to antiquarian book dealers with Web sites, including many international booksellers as well as the Antiquarian Booksellers Association of America, among many others. Besides linking to out-of-print book dealers, Bookwire also provides links to publisher sites, author tour information, reviews, and links to many other aspects of book publishing and selling.

3.3 Internet Resources for Out-of-Print Books

3.3.1 Metasearch Engines

These out-of-print sites can be used to search more than one of the major out-of-print databases simultaneously.

(a) AddALL: http://www.addall.com/used

AddALL is a free website and search engine built by book buyers for book buyers. You presently can search AddALL for the book listings of 41 online stores. Price, preferred currency, and shipping information are available for titles searched. AddALL simultaneously searches the following out-of-print databases: Abebooks, Alibris, AntiqBook,

Biblion, Bibliology, Bibliopoly, Biblioroom, Chapitre, Ele-
phantBooks, Half.com, ILAB, Maremagnum, Powell's.
  (b) Bookfinder: http://www.bookfinder.com
      This search engine was developed by Anirvan Chatterjee,
      a former graduate student at the University of California,
      Berkeley. Bookfinder's search engine allows you to si-
      multaneously search the following out-of-print database
      sites: Abebooks, ABooksearch.com, Alibris, AntiqBook,
      BiblioDirect, Biblion, Bibliology, Bibliopoly, bigger-
      books.com, BookAvenue.com, Books and Collectibles,
      ChooseBooks, ecampus.com, ElephantBooks, Global
      Book Mart, Half.com, JustBooks, Maremagnum, Popula,
      Powell's, TextbooksX.com, TomFolio.com, Used Book
      Central. Searching can be limited by binding type, price,
      first edition, or signed copy. Keyword searching is avail-
      able.

3.3.2 Out-of-Print Book Online Web Databases and Electronic
      Sources
      The following list of out-of-print online databases is a repre-
      sentative sample of the best known and easiest to use web-
      sites available for the location of out-of-print materials. This
      list is by no means a complete listing of out-of-print databases.

  (a) Advanced Book Exchange (Abebooks): http://www
      .abebooks.com
      Well organized and easy to search by author, title, and
      keyword. The searcher can limit by bookstore location,
      binding type, and attributes such as first edition, signed,
      dust jacket, language, and price. Abebooks also allows
      you to browse by subject, topic, bookseller specialty, or
      geographic location. A searcher can register and list up to
      500 wants for free and can place orders directly through
      the out-of-print bookseller holding the needed title. In
      most cases, payment by credit card is preferred, although
      some booksellers will ship books with an invoice, if you
      request it.
  (b) Alibris: http://www.alibris.com
      Formerly known as Interloc, this database was originally
      accessible only by subscription. Alibris purports to be

"the ultimate source for out-of-print and rare books."
Among its affiliated partners are Amazon.com, Bor-
ders.com, and Barnes and Noble. They offer a 100 percent guarantee on all books purchased. Searching can be
done on title, author, subject, publisher, ISBN, and keyword. Searches may be limited by price, binding, lan-
guage, etc. Libraries purchasing from Alibris may set up
an account to purchase books using a credit card or purchase order.

(c) Amazon Books: http://www.amazon.com
Amazon at one time billed itself as "Earth's biggest bookstore." Today they offer 4.7 million books, CDs, audio-
books, DVDs, computer games, and more online. Recently, Amazon acquired Exchange.com and with it
Bibliofind.com. Books can be searched for by author, title, subject, and keyword. Amazon will search for out-of-
print titles and notify buyers via e-mail.

(d) Biblion: http://www.biblion.com
This United Kingdom–based site has over 1,000 dealers
selling the best of British books. Books can be searched
by author, title, publisher, and keyword, and limited by
date of publication, first edition, signed, and price (in
pounds Sterling).

(e) Bookavenue.com: http://www.bookavenue.com
Bookavenue states that it offers "great books at fair
prices." Their website states: "Buy from the people who
have the books on hand at substantial savings from other
sites." Books can be searched by author, title, seller, category, and "supersearch." Wants can be listed for free.

(f) France Antiques: http://www.franceantiq.fr
Approximately 57 antiquarian booksellers located in vari-
ous areas of France offer rare and out-of-print books for
sale. Titles can be searched only by keywords that link to
a bookseller's catalog listings. France Antique also offers
a free search service.

(g) Powell's Books: http://www.powells.com
Powell's slogan is, "You won't find a larger selection of
used, rare, and out-of-print books anywhere. Period."
Powell's combined locations house over 1.5 million books
and this vast inventory is searchable via the Web. Books

can be searched by keywords, title, author, publisher, and ISBN. Powell's will search for out-of-print books not in their stock for free.

(h) UKBookWorld: http://UKBookWorld.com
The British marketplace for scholarly and collectible old, rare, and out-of-print books. You can search by author, title, publisher, date and subject and limit your searches by price. You can create a free account to list up to 50 wants. Wants are listed by author or subject, not individual title. The company checks wants daily and sends you notifications via e-mail.

3.3.3 Out-of-Print Online Mailing List Sources

Online mailing lists, also known as Listservs, are accessed via e-mail subscription. Subscribers post to and receive all posted messages via e-mail. Many lists provide a digest format that groups together messages and sends them as a single e-mail message. Lists of out-of-print wants can be posted to the list so that dealers can respond.

(a) Antiqbook
Provides a forum for individuals involved in the out-of-print and antiquarian book trade, including booksellers, librarians, and book collectors. This list has a strong European focus and is based in the Netherlands. Subscribers list books to buy and sell as well as bibliographical questions, announcements, etc. The cost of subscription is free for noncommercial users, $15 for all others. To subscribe, go to the Antiqbook website (http://www.antiqbook.com/mailinglists/antiqbookform.html) and submit the subscription form found there.

(b) ACQNET
ACQNET is a moderated list for acquisitions librarians and others interested in acquisitions. Postings may not be made directly but must be submitted to the editor, Eleanor Cook, at cookie@appstate.edu. The list may be used to exchange information, ideas, share solutions to problems as well as to make inquiries regarding booksellers, both new and used. Commercial postings are not accepted. To subscribe to ACQNET, send the following message to listproc@listproc.appstate.edu:

subscribe acqnet-l [yourfirstname] [yourlastname]
Do not put anything else in the message. Additional information regarding the list can be found on the AcqWeb website (see Section 3.2 1).

(c) Biblio: The Bibliophile Mailing List
Familiarly known as Biblio, this mailing list was created for buying and selling rare, scarce, out-of-print, and collectible books. List members share information on a variety of book-related topics. This is a closed list and only subscribers may post. The cost of a subscription is $30 per year. For more information, contact the list owner, Lynn DeWeese-Parkinson, at cldp@teleport.com; 2620 8th Ave., Forest Grove, OR 97116; (503) 359-0846.

3.4 Using In-Print Book Vendors for Out-of-Print Searching

3.4.1 Choosing an Appropriate Vendor

(a) Length of time vendor will search for an out-of-print title—Longer searches often result in higher success rates.
(b) Rate of success in locating out-of-print titles—The number of different sources a vendor uses, traditional as well as electronic, can have an impact on the rate of success in locating titles.
(c) Ability to locate foreign as well as domestically published titles.
(d) Percent of markup on prices—Vendors charge 50 to 100 percent more than the cost of purchasing a book directly from an out-of-print book dealer.

3.4.2 Setting Price Limits and Book Condition

(a) To speed up the process of acquiring out-of-print titles via a vendor, a price limit may be set in advance for which a confirmation by the library is not needed prior to purchase, e.g., books under $50 will be sent without contacting the library to confirm the item's price.
(b) Acceptable condition of books to be purchased should also be set in advance with the vendor. For example, the library will accept books in very good condition with light underlining but no highlighting.

3.4.3 List of Some In-Print Vendors That Do Out-of-Print Searching

> (a) Alfred Jaeger, Inc.
> (b) Amazon.com
> (c) Aux Amateur de Livres
> (d) Blackwell's Book Service
> (e) Casalini
> (f) Otto Harrassowitz
> (g) International Service Company
> (h) Midwest Library Service, Inc.
> (i) OPAMP Technical Books, Inc.

3.5   Print-on-Demand Services

The advent of new technologies, such as high-speed printers, and electronic files, has led to the creation of publishing service providers that are able to offer printing "on demand." What "on demand" means is that these service providers are able to reprint a single copy of a copyright-cleared book or serial on request. Generally, for reprinting an out-of-stock title to be cost effective, a publisher must wait for a large number of orders of the title. New technologies, such as the IBM and Oce printers, have made printing one copy of a book both cost effective and effortless. The quality of print on-demand books and serials can vary greatly depending on the quality of the original source for the reproduction as well as the equipment used in the reproduction process. The following publishing service providers are some of the businesses currently offering this service.

3.5.1 Backinprint.com: http://www.backinprint.com
Backinprint.com is associated with the Authors Guild. They are dedicated to making out-of-print books more readily available to readers. Readers can easily find and order out-of-print titles online, by mail, or by a toll-free phone number. Shakespeare & Co., a New York City bookseller, will fulfill orders for these books.
Shakespeare & Co. Booksellers, 138 Watts Street, New York, NY 10013; (212) 965-9093; (212) 965-9684 fax.

3.5.2 Lightning Source, Inc.: http://www.lightningsource.com
Lightning Source is a subsidiary of Ingram Industries, Inc. They offer a digital fulfillment service that includes conver-

sion, storage, management, and distribution of digital content. Lightning Source has a digital library of over 16,000 titles, growing by an average of 400 titles per week. Their plan is to add another 50,000 titles. On-demand printing has a turn-around time of 48 hours per title.

Lightning Source, Inc., 1246 Heil Quaker Blvd., La Vergne, TN 37086; (615) 213-5815; (615) 213-4426 fax.

3.5.3 UMI Books on Demand: http://wwwlib.umi.com/bod

Bell and Howell's Books on Demand offers approximately 150,000 out-of-print books for black-and-white reproduction in either paper- or hard-bound cover. A searchable database of the titles available can be found at their website along with an order form.

Bell and Howell Information and Learning, 300 North Zeeb Road, P.O. Box 1346, Ann Arbor, MI 48106-1346; 1-800-889-3358.

3.5.4 Xlibris: http://www.xlibris.com

Xlibris is a partner of Random House ventures. They act as a service provider for authors wishing to publish their own books or to affordably republish out-of-print works to which they have reclaimed their rights.

Xlibris, 436 Walnut St., 11th floor, Philadelphia, PA 19106; 1-888-795-4274; info@xlibris.com.

3.6 Buying Newer and Remaindered Editions

Printing overruns and leftover copies of new titles are often sold off by the publisher at cost to remainder houses in order to eliminate the cost of warehousing these additional copies. Numerous book-stores, such as Barnes and Noble, Strand, and Powell's, carry re-maindered books. In addition, there are now a number of websites where remaindered books can be found. The following is a list of some of them.

3.6.1 BookCloseOuts: http://www.bookcloseouts.com

BookCloseOuts claims that it is the "best seller" in bargain books, offering from 50 to 90 percent off of list prices for ti-tles. The site is very easy to use and can be searched by key-word, title, author, ISBN, and publisher. You can also browse by category, author, or publisher or look at new arrivals. There really are bargains to be had here.

3.6.2 Book Depot: http://www.bookdepot.com
This is supposed to be one of North America's largest whole-salers of discount and remaindered books, with five million books in-stock. A quick search may be performed using title, author, publisher, ISBN or keyword. You can also browse by category, author, or publisher. A credit card is necessary to make purchases and there is a $250.00 order minimum.

3.6.3 Half.com: http://half.ebay.comhttp://www.half.com
Half.com offers not only used books, but CDs, videotapes, DVDs, and games. Prices can be unbelievably low but the condition of an item is not always completely described. Past customers rate their satisfaction with a seller's service and with the item purchased from the seller. You can also sign up to sell your own items on this site. Books may be searched by title, author, keyword, and ISBN. Half.com has recently been purchased by eBay.

4. Audiovisual Materials

The formats of audiovisual materials have seen drastic changes over the years. Many of them are no longer being produced. This guide will focus on only the main types of audiovisual materials that libraries are actively seeking today.

4.1 Videos and DVDs

This section deals with sources for locating videotapes and DVDs. While some libraries may collect 16 millimeter motion picture film, by and large they are very specialized libraries; therefore this guide does not cover this type of material.

The American Film Institute (AFI) offers (as of June 8, 2002) the following tips for locating hard-to-find films on their website (http://www.afi.com):

1. Learn as much about the film as you can. Each piece of infor-mation may produce a lead.
2. Use the standard search engines with the information, not just the title. Often these searches can lead to the website of a com-pany that distributes the film.

3. For mainstream Hollywood films the original production company is not always the company that owns the film. Early MGM films are owned by AOL-Time Warner, because Time Warner acquired them when they bought Turner, which had acquired them when Turner purchased MGM.
4. Just because you saw it once or read about it does not mean it still exists or is available. The first Super Bowl and the premiere of *The Tonight Show* are both considered "lost" by archivists. Of the more than 21,000 feature-length films produced in the United States before 1951, only half exist today.
5. There is no magic database of all films ever made and where you can buy the video.

4.1.1 Video/Motion Picture Organizations

(a) American Film Institute (AFI): http://www.afi.com
Established in 1967, AFI is dedicated to advancing and preserving the art of the moving image. AFI offers tips and lists of websites for locating films and hard-to-find and rare video. Includes Louis B. Mayer Library.

(b) Association of Moving Image Archivists (AMIA): http://www.amianet.org
The AMIA is a professional association established to advance the field of moving image archiving by fostering cooperation among individuals and organizations concerned with the collection, description, preservation, exhibition and use of moving image materials.

(c) National Film Preservation Board: http://www.loc.gov/film/ National Film Preservation Foundation (NFPF): http://www.filmpreservation.org
The National Film Preservation Board, established by the National Film Preservation Act of 1988, implements the National Film Preservation Plan whereby each year 25 "culturally, historically or aesthetically significant films" are chosen for the National Film Registry. The National Film Preservation Foundation was established in conjunction with the National Film Preservation Board in 1997 to support preservation activities nationwide. Sites contain location of film archives and the National Film Registry.

4.1.2 Directories and Indexes for Video and DVDs

(a) Print Directories
Print directories, published annually, can help determine
if the film you are seeking is available on video.

1. *Bowker's Complete Video Directory*
Currently a four-volume set containing information on
over 250,000 titles. Provides information on entertain-
ment and educational video, including foreign lan-
guage titles and silent movies. Current cost is $325.00
for the set. For additional information contact: R.R.
Bowker, P.O. Box 32, New Providence, NJ 07974; 1-
800-521-8110; customerservice@bowker.com.

2. *Leonard Maltin's Movie and Video Guide*
Concise reference guide providing an alphabetical list
of films along with their description, ratings, stars, and
other information such as running time, director, and
format (e.g., VHS, DVD, laserdisc). Current cost is
$20.00. For additional information contact: Dutton/
Plume, 405 Murray Hill Parkway, East Rutherford, NJ
07073-2136; 1-800-788-6262; online@penguinputnam
.com.

3. *VideoHound's Golden Movie Retriever*
Contains 23,000 movie reviews and nine indexes, including a useful and fun category list. Birth and death
dates have been added to the cast and director indexes. Has lists of video sources and useful websites.
Current cost is $21.95. For additional information con-
tact: Gale Group, P.O. Box 9187, Farmington Hills, MI
48333-9187; 1-800-877-4253; 1-800-414-5043 fax;
galeord@galegroup.com.

4. *Video Source Book*
Provides a fairly comprehensive annual guide to
videos, which extends beyond feature films to include classroom aids, corporate training programs,
technical resources, self-help guides, children's features, documentaries, and more. The book is
arranged alphabetically by title with six indexes: al-

ternate title, subject, credits, awards, special formats and program distributors. Each entry provides a description of the program and information on how to obtain copies. The current list price of the 29th edition (2002) is $380. For additional information contact: Gale Group, P.O. Box 9187, Farmington Hills, MI 48333-9187; 1-800-877-4253; 1-800-414-5043 fax; gale-ord@galegroup.com.

(b) Web Directories
1. Internet Movie Database (IMDb): http://www.imdb.com Searchable Web database that contains a vast collection of movie information, including who was in a movie, who made it, filming locations, trivia, and where you can find reviews, fan sites, and more. Offers links to sites for purchasing films on video.
2. Library of Congress Motion Picture and Television Reading Room: http://www.loc.gov/rr/mopic/
The Library of Congress operates the Reading Room to provide access and information services to researchers. The Library of Congress provides duplication of audio and moving image materials in their collections if all the copyright restrictions to these materials have been cleared. Includes lists of films at the Library of Congress and finding aids. American Memory Online Films are accessible from this site.

4.1.3 Internet Sources for Used and Out-of-Distribution Video and DVD

(a) Amazon.com: http://www.amazon.com
The video segment of Amazon is linked to a large number of used and out-of-distribution video vendors and stores. Users who do a general search under "video" often find used (or sometimes new wholesale) copies of in- or out-of-distribution titles. A credit card is required for purchase.

(b) Amazon Europe: http://www.amazon.co.uk (United Kingdom), http://www.amazon.co.fr (France), http://www.amazon.co.de (Denmark)

Because of the complex nature of feature film distribution, many films, both U.S. and foreign, are released abroad but not in the United States. Amazon Europe serves as a primary source for these materials. It should be noted that materials purchased via Amazon Europe are generally in not U.S. video format, i.e. PAL or SECAM.

(c) Video Oyster: http://www.videooyster.com/store/
Large inventory of used and out-of-distribution tapes. An excellent source for rare materials, although prices tend to be on the high side.

(d) eBay: http://www.ebay.com
The Web's ubiquitous, all-purpose auction site. eBay posts a large number of both in- and out-of-distribution videos and DVDs. Because eBay is a commercial site and does not closely supervise auctions, the buyer must always be wary of illegal copies. Prices are based on competitive bidding. Payment frequently requires either a check or credit card payment through third party services, such as PayPal. Many online vendors now offer a "Buy It Now" feature for those who absolutely *must* have an item and don't want to go through the anxiety and time involved in bidding on an object.

(e) Distribution Video (DVA): http://www.dva.com
Large inventory of both new and previously viewed videos and DVDs. DVA will search for specifically requested titles. All previously viewed materials are guaranteed for the life of the tape or disc.

(f) Mike LeBell's Video
This video shop is known for finding hard-to-find videos. For additional information contact: 75 Fremont Place, Los Angeles, CA 90005; (213) 938-3333; (213) 938-3334 fax; MLVIDEO@aol.com.

4.1.4 Online Mailing List Sources for Out-of-Distribution Videos and DVDs
Online video mailing lists can be an excellent resource for locating distributors, hard-to-find videos and DVDs, as well as discussions on related topics such as copyright and intellectual property issues, library/vendor relations, etc. The following online mailing lists represent the most widely used resources.

(a) VIDEOLIB

Serves as an effective "working tool" for video librarians by encouraging the lively discussion of issues relating to the selection, evaluation, acquisition, bibliographic control, preservation, and use of current and evolving video formats in libraries and related institutions. It is an unmoderated list. To subscribe, send the message "subscribe videolib your name" to listserv@library.berkeley.edu. To contribute to the list after subscribing, send your message to videolib@library.berkeley.edu. For further information go to http://www.lib.berkeley.edu/VideoLib/ or contact Gary Handman, ghandman@library.berkeley.edu.

(b) VIDEONEWS

Serves as an electronic clearinghouse for information about new services, products, resources, and programs of interest to video librarians and archivists, educators, and others involved in the selection, acquisition, programming, and preservation of video materials in nonprofit settings. The VIDEONEWS online mailing list is sponsored by the American Library Association Video Round Table. To subscribe, send the message "subscribe videonews your name" to listserv@library.berkeley.edu. To contribute to the list after subscribing, send your message to videonews@library.berkeley.edu. For further information go to http://www.lib.berkeley.edu/VideoLib/ or contact Gary Handman, ghandman@library.berkeley.edu.

4.2 Sound Recordings

These listings identify some of the best known and easiest to use sources of out-of-print sound recordings. The dealer listings are grouped by method (search services, Web databases, Internet lists) and include notes on particular specialties. These may involve format (compact disc, vinyl LP, 78) as well as genre (such as classical, jazz, musical theater). Some are specialists in service to libraries and that is noted as well.

4.2.1 Music and Sound Recording Organizations

(a) Association of Recorded Sound Collections: http://www.arsc-audio.org/

Nonprofit organization dedicated to information exchange on all aspects of recorded sound. Members include dealers, appraisers, archivists, and librarians. An online mailing list is available; to subscribe, see http://www.arsc-audio.org/arsclist.html.

(b) Music Library Association: http://www.musiclibrary assoc.org/

Members include people informed and experienced in the realm of out-of-print music acquisitions and all aspects of music in libraries. An online mailing list is available; to subscribe, see http://www.musiclibraryassoc.org/useful/use.htm.

4.2.2 Directories and Indexes for Out-of-Print Sound Recordings

(a) Print Directories

1. *Fanfare: The Magazine for Serious Record Collectors* (ISSN 0148-9364. Six issues/year, $39) Their classified page offers useful listings of dealers, largely classical.
2. *Goldmine: The Collectors' Record and Compact Disc Marketplace* (ISSN 1055-2685. 26 issues/year, $39.95) Advertisements and stock listings for a large array of used and collectible dealers, mostly (but not exclusively) of pop music.
3. *Notes: Quarterly Journal of the Music Library Association* (ISSN 0027-4380. Six issues/year, $70) Back-of-the-book classified advertising section can include specialist out-of-print dealers and search services who understand service to libraries.

(b) Web Directories:

1. Classical Recordings Collection Building, Label Pages, and Dealers: http://www.lib.washington.edu/music/classicaldisco.html
John Gibbs' (University of Washington) directory of Web resources for librarians and other collection developers includes a section on used records and 78s. A

related site, *Early or Historical Sound Recordings Collections and Other 78 & Cylinder Sites of Interest,* is located at http://www.lib.washington.edu/music/records.html.

2. Used Classical CDs Meta-list: http://gateway.library.uiuc.edu/mux/usedcds.htm
   Leslie Troutman's (University of Illinois) very useful Web directory focuses on the classical genre and the CD format. Enhanced by comments from members of the Music Library Association.

3. Web Resources for Out-of-Print Sound Recordings: http://aseaberg.home.mindspring.com/opmusic.html
   Companion piece to the *ALCTS Guide to Out-of-Print Materials*; updated regularly by co-author Anna Seaburg.

4. Yahoo Commercial Directory: Used CDs, Records, and Tapes: http://dir.yahoo.com/Business_and_Economy/Shopping_and_Services/Music/CDs_Records_and_Tapes/Used/
   Alphabetical list of retailer sites; worth a look. Like all of Yahoo, the sites are self-nominated.

4.2.3 Search Services and Places to List Active Wants

(a) A-1 Record Finders: http://www.aonerecordfinders.com
   Offers an inventory of over 1,000,000 titles in vinyl LP and 45 formats, which they will search at no obligation to the requestor. Specialists in sound tracks and shows. For additional information contact: A-1 Record Finders, 5639 Melrose Ave., Los Angeles, CA 90038; (323) 732-6737; (818) 841-8708 fax; a1recordfind@earthlink.net.

(b) Amazon.com: http://www.amazon.com
   Offers a finding service. Fill out a form specifying desired titles and an end date; a number of out-of-print dealers will search. All genres, all formats.

(c) CD Trackdown: http://www.cdtrackdown.com
   Form-driven search service for out-of-print, overseas, and other hard-to-find CDs, mainly classical. Offers a well-designed query form (composer, title of piece, opus number/key, title of album, performers, instrument, orchestra,

conductor, record label, catalog number). A service of Rhinebeck Records, specialists in service to libraries; purchase orders accepted. For additional information contact: CD Trackdown, c/o Rhinebeck Records, P.O. Box 262, Salt Point, NY 12578; (845) 266-3500; (845) 266-4432 fax; rhinebeckrecords@compuserve.com.

(d) Harold Moores Records: http://www.haroldmoores.com
London-based, specialist, classical music store whose point of pride is a stock of 70,000 vinyl LPs in excellent condition. Notably tenacious. For additional information contact: Harold Moores Records, 2 Gt. Marlborough St., London W1V 1DE, United Kingdom; +44 (20) 7437 1576; +44 (20) 7287 0377 fax; sales@hmrecords.demon.co.uk.

(e) Yankee Music Search: http://www.yankeemusic.com
Form-based search service for sound recordings in all musical genres and all formats ("CDs, cassettes, LPs, 45s, 78s, even the occasional 8-track"). Specify two-week or open-ended search. For additional information contact: Yankee Music Search, P.O. Box 1143, Flushing, NY 11354; (718) 463-1702; (718) 463-8480 fax; info@yankeemusic.com.

(f) *Goldmine: The Collectors' Record and Compact Disc Marketplace*
(See Directories and Indexes above.) Includes a want list section.

4.2.4 Web Databases of Out-of-Print Sound Recordings

(a) Berkshire Record Outlet: http://www.berkshirerecordoutlet.com/
Cutouts (remainders) of CDs in all genres, especially classical. Full text keyword search; filter by label, format, or (usefully) price. For additional information contact: Berkshire Record Outlet, RR 1, Lee, MA 01238; 1-800-992-1200; (413) 243-4340 fax; berkrec@vgernet.net.

(b) CDChoice: http://cdchoice.com
Search or browse a large database of classical and jazz CDs; genuinely useful search form has well-thought-out access points. Search by artist or composer, title, catalog

number, soloist, conductor, or ensemble or orchestra. Specialists in institutional ordering; purchase orders accepted. For additional information contact: CDChoice, (215) 988-1400; (215) 988-9828 fax; cdchoice@pobox.com.

(c) GEMM: http://www.gemm.com
"Global Electronic Music Marketplace," a database aggregator, searches the stock of more than 5,000 used sound recordings dealers worldwide—16 million items in all genres and formats. Search by artist, album title, label, catalog number, or category; filter by format, price, condition, or country of manufacture. Want-list service is also available. Nonpareil as a large listing of dealer and collector stock, but listings (contributed by sellers) make use of highly variable terminology. Genuinely international in scope with mirror sites in Japanese, Spanish, German, Dutch.

4.2.5 Internet Lists of Out-of-Print Sound Recordings

(a) Hancock and Monks: http://www.hancockandmonks.co.uk
UK-based music shop with extensive stock of new and secondhand classical CDs, books on music, scores and sheet music. Also carries a wide range of classic films and opera on video and DVD, as well as a comprehensive stock of spoken-word cassettes and CDs. Browseable stock listings, organized alphabetically by composer. For additional information contact: Hancock and Monks, 15 Broad Street, Hay-on-Wye, HR3 5DB, United Kingdom; jerry@hancockandmonks.co.uk.

(b) Loran Records: http://www.loranrecords.com
Specialists in vinyl LPs of all musical genres, with over 40,000 in stock. Well-organized classified lists include informative notes on condition and reasonable prices. Also offers a search service. For additional information contact: Loran Records, P.O. Box 1604, Florissant, MO 63031; (314) 921-2649; (314) 921-4091 fax; loranrec@aol.com.

(c) Parnassus Records: http://www.parnassusrecords.com
Extensive monthly listings of out-of-print classical and jazz CDs, as well as vinyl LPs. Catalogs are available online or

in print; their "Silver and Gold" catalog includes out-of-print and imported classical (and some jazz) CDs; "Parnassus Select" lists classical and jazz vinyl LPs. Also offers a search service. For additional information contact: Parnassus Records, 51 Goat Hill Road, Saugerties, NY 12477-3008; (845) 246-3332; (845) 246-6584 fax; parnassus@ulster.net.

(d) Recordfinders.com: http://www.recordfinders.com
Virginia-based,175,000 item catalog is both browsable and searchable, and includes fixed-price as well as auction items. Filterable by format (45, 78, LP). For additional information contact: Recordfinders.com, P.O. Box 1047, Glen Allen, VA 23060; (804) 266-1154; (804) 264-9660 fax; sales1@recordfinders.com.

4.2.6. Online Auction Sources for Out-of-Print Sound Recordings

(a) eBay: http://pages.ebay.com/catindex/music.html
Large online auction of CDs, records, tapes, sheet music, and memorabilia, along with everything else. Database of offerings is browsable by format and genre, or searchable by keyword based on seller's description.

(b) Nauck's Vintage Records: http://www.78rpm.com
Reliable auction dealer for 78s and cylinders, including blues, gospel, classical, operatic, hillbilly, Cajun, historical, political, jazz, dance bands, rhythm and blues, rock and roll, foreign, ethnic, personality, and comedy recordings. Also picture discs, children's records, Edison Diamond Discs, rare labels, radio transcriptions and novelty records. For additional information contact: Nauck's Vintage Records, 323 Inway Dr., Spring, TX 77389-3643; (425) 930-6862; nauck@78rpm.com.

(c) Norbeck, Peters, and Ford: http://www.norpete.com
Notable classical (especially opera) specialists select and sell 78s, LPs, and CDs of historical worth in service to an anti-mediocrity ethos. For additional information contact: Norbeck, Peters, and Ford, P.O. Box 210, Swanton, VT 05488-0210; (802) 868-9300; (802) 868-9302 fax; norpete@aol.com.

5. Serials

5.1 Traditional Means of Acquiring Out-of-Print Serials

Prior to the Web, librarians acquired back issues of serials (journals, magazines, and newspapers) through purchasing microforms of those items, working with serials backfile dealers, or maintaining paper lists of missing serials issues. All of these methods are still used to acquire missing serials.

5.1.1 Microforms

The following companies provide microform copies of most of the more common serials available for purchase.

(a) Lexis-Nexis Academic and Library Solutions: http://www .lexisnexis.com/academic

Provides archival microfiche for a broad range of publications from 1789 to the present. Includes the Congressional Information Service, Inc. (CIS), collection of government documents as well as the University Publications of America papers and reports collections, such as the Holocaust Era Research Collection and the Native American Studies collection. For additional information contact: 4520 East-West Highway, Bethesda, MD 20814; 1-800-638-8380; (301) 657-3203 fax; academicinfo@lexisnexis.com.

(b) Primary Source Microfilm:http://www.galegroup.com/psm

Primary Source Microfilm, an imprint of the Gale Group, provides a specialized collection of primary research sources, such as the *Times* (London) from 1785 forward; the Goldsmiths'-Kress Library of Economic Literature, early English newspapers, etc. For additional information contact: 12 Lunar Drive, Woodbridge, CT 06525-2398; 1-800-444-0799; (203) 397-3893 fax; sales@gale.com.

(c) ProQuest Information and Learning: http://www.umi.com

Features the UMI and Chadwyck-Healey microform collections. The UMI collection contains over 19,000 distinct periodicals and 7,000 newspapers from around the world. For additional information contact: 300 N. Zeeb Road, P.O. Box 1346, Ann Arbor, MI 48106-1346; 1-800-521-0600; 1-800-308-1586 fax; info@il.proquest.com.

5.1.2 Serials Backfile Dealers
The following are two of the more prominent serials backfile dealers that sell back issues of out-of-print serials.

(a) Alfred Jaeger, Inc.: http://www.ajaeger.com
Has an inventory of over 40,000 titles and will search for out-of-print and difficult-to-find titles. Requests for titles can be made by regular mail, e-mail, or telephone. They sell single issues or complete volumes and accept payment by credit card, check, or invoice. For additional information contact: 66 Austin Blvd., P.O. Box 9009, Commack, NY 11725-9009; 1-800-969-5247; (631) 545-1537 fax; jaeger@ajaeger.com.

(b) Schmidt Periodicals GmbH and Periodicals Service Company: http://www.periodicals.com
These two companies have joined to provide access to more than three million volumes in all subject areas. They are a major reprinter of academic journals and also supply backsets of journals, series, and reference works. They can supply single issues, volumes, or partial sets. Their website contains a database of their stock that is both browsable and searchable. For additional information contact:
Schmidt Periodicals GmbH, Dettendorf Romerring 12, D-83075 Bad Feilnbach, Germany; +00 (49) 8064 221; +00 (49) 8064 557; schmidt@backsets.com.
Periodicals Service Company, Attn: John Mullin, 11 Main Street, Germantown, NY 12526; (518) 537-4700; (518) 537-5899 fax; psc@periodicals.com.

5.2 Serials Backfile Exchange Organizations

The following two organizations were developed to provide libraries with a way to obtain copies of out-of-print serials as well as to dispose of their duplicate issues, and at the same time benefit other libraries in need.

5.2.1 Duplicates Exchange Union (DEU): http://www.ala.org/alcts, click Publications, Duplicates Exchange Union
The Duplicates Exchange Union is an online mailing list main-

tained by the Association for Library Collections and Technical Services. It facilitates the exchange of lists of available duplicate items among member libraries free of charge. There is no membership fee nor requirement of American Library Association membership; however, libraries that join the organization must agree to issue at least one exchange list per year. Libraries looking for a copy of a missing serial must scan the lists sent by other member libraries and then contact the library offering the item. Participating libraries do not charge each other for materials but refund the postage costs for the materials they receive from other participating libraries. For additional information contact: Association for Library Collections and Technical Services, American Library Association, 50 East Huron Street, Chicago, IL 60611; (312) 280-5034.

5.2.2 United States Book Exchange (USBE): http://www.usbe.com
    The United States Book Exchange (USBE) is a 60-year-old nonprofit organization with over 17,000 titles and 5 million back issues available. USBE has two membership categories, one has a $150 fee and a charge of $7.00 per back issue; the other is free but charges $20.00 per back issue. Titles of serials can be searched online. Orders can be placed online, by fax, or by mail. For additional information contact: 2969 West 25th Street, Cleveland, OH 44113; (216) 241-6960; (216) 241-6966 fax; info@usbe.com.

5.3 Serials Backfile Internet Mailing List Sources

Internet-based e-mail lists provide libraries with an opportunity to exchange or purchase back issues and/or volumes of missing serials that are no longer available in print. The following lists represent some of the most commonly used exchange lists.

5.3.1 Backserv
    Devoted to the informal exchange of serial back issues and books among libraries. Serials back issues and books in all nonmedical subject areas that are needed may be listed. This is not a discussion list. Subscribers wishing to discuss the process of exchanging materials or dealers are requested to post messages on SERIALST or ACQNET. Medical materials may be exchanged on the Backmed list (see below). To subscribe to Backserv go the SwetsBlackwell website at

http://lists.swetsblackwell.com/mailman/listinfo/backserv.
The lists archives are available athttp://lists.swetsblackwell
.com/pipermail/backserv/.

5.3.2 Backmed
Devoted to the informal exchange of medical serials back issues and books among libraries. It provides a forum for the
listing of both available and wanted items in primarily medical
subject areas. To subscribe to Backmed go the SwetsBlack-
well website at http://lists.swetsblackwell.com/mailman/
listinfo/backmed.

5.3.3 Euroback
List for the free exchange of duplicate serials back issues and
books among European libraries. To subscribe, send a message
saying "subscribe euroback" to majordomo@lists.ulg.ac.be. The
proprietors of the list are Paul Thirion (paul.thirion@ulg.ac.be)
and Simone Jerome (sjerome@ulg.ac.be).

5.3.4 Local and National Organizations
Often libraries with duplicate or deaccessioned serials will
post e-mail messages to their local organization's list to see if
another library can use the items. Postage reimbursement for
mailing the items is usually expected.

5.3.5 SERIALST (Serials in Libraries Discussion Forum)
Provides a forum for topics in serials processing, including:
cataloging, acquisitions, collection management, serials budg-
eting and pricing, binding, preservation, microfilm and other
nonprint serials media, union list activities, announcements,
news, and job postings. This list is not a forum for the trade or
exchange of duplicate, unwanted, or wanted serials, however,
information may be obtained regarding serials vendors. The
list is moderated and messages are reviewed prior to posting.
To subscribe, send a message saying "subscribe serialst your-
firstname yourlastname" (i.e., subscribe serialst Jane Doe) to
listserv@list.uvm. Additional information regarding the list
can be found at http://www.uvm.edu/~bmaclenn/serialst.html.

5.4 Print-on-Demand Services

Through the use of new technologies, some vendors are now offering high-resolution reproductions of journal issues. Here are a few:

5.4.1 Back-in-Print

Launched in 1995 as a joint venture by the University of Toronto Library, the University of Toronto Press, and ISM Library Information Services, Back-in-Print offers digital copies that can then be used to create print copies of out-of-print books and serials held by the University of Toronto Library. All copies are made in compliance with copyright laws. For additional information contact: Back-in-Print, University of Toronto Press, 214 College Street, Toronto, Ontario, Canada M5T 3A1; (416) 978-7927; (416) 978-7242 fax; backinprint@ utpress.utoronto.ca.

5.4.2 Schmidt Periodicals GmbH and Periodicals Service Company

Providers of journal reprints as well as back issues. (See 5.1.2b for complete contact information.)

Out-of-Print Materials URL Resource List

1) Organizations—National and International
   a) Books
      (1) Antiquarian Booksellers of America Association (ABAA): http://abaa.org
      (2) International League of Antiquarian Booksellers (ILAB): http://www.ilab-lila.com
      (3) International Book Collectors Association (IBCA): http://www.rarebooks.org
   b) Motion Pictures
      (1) American Film Institute (AFI): http://www.afi.com
      (2) Association of Moving Image Archivists (AMIA): http://www.amianet.org
      (3) National Film Preservation Board: http://lcWeb.loc.gov/film
      (4) National Film Preservation Foundation (NFPF): http://www.filmpreservation.org
   c) Sound Recordings
      (1) Association of Recorded Sound Collections: http://www.arsc-audio.org
      (2) Music Library Association: http://www.musiclibrary assoc.org
   d) Serials
      (1) Duplicates Exchange Union (DEU): http://www.ala.org/alcts/publications/deu.html
      (2) United States Book Exchange (USBE): http://www.usbe.com

2) Directories—Web-based
   a) Books
      (1) AcqWeb: http://acqWeb.library.vanderbilt.edu
      (2) Books and Book Collecting: http://www.trussel.com/
           f_booksx.htm
      (3) Bookwire: http://www.bookwire.com/bookwire/
           booksellers/antiquarian-booksellers.html
   b) Motion Pictures
      (1) Internet Movie Database (IMDb): http://www.imdb.com
      (2) Library of Congress Motion Picture and Television Read-
           ing Room: http://lcWeb.loc.gov/rr/mopic
   c) Sound Recordings
      (1) Classical Recordings Collection Building, Label Pages,
           and Dealers: http://www.lib.washington.edu/music/
           classicaldisco.html
      (2) Used Classical CDs Meta-list: http://gateway.library.uiuc
           .edu/mux/usedcds.htm
      (3) Web Resources for Out-of-Print Sound Recordings:
           http://aseaberg.home.mindspring.com/opmusic.html
      (4) Yahoo Commercial Directory: Used CDs, Records, and
           Tapes: http://dir.yahoo.com/Business_and_Economy/
           Shopping_and_Services/Music/CDs__Records__and_
           Tapes/Used/
3) Search Engines and Databases:
   a) General
      (1) Amazon.com can be used to search for all out-of-
           print/out-of-distribution material.
           (a) United States: http://www.amazon.com
           (b) United Kingdom: http://www.amazon.co.uk
           (c) France: http://www.amazon.co.fr
           (d) Denmark: http://www.amazon.co.de
      (2) e-Bay auctions out-of-print books and audio-visual ma-
           terials: http://www.ebay.com
   b) Books
      (1) AddALL: http://www.addall.com/used
      (2) Advanced Book Exchange: http://www.abebooks.com
      (3) Alibris: http://www.alibris.com
      (4) Biblion: http://www.biblion.com
      (5) Bookavenue.com: http://www.bookavenue.com
      (6) BookCloseOuts: http://www.bookcloseouts.com

(7) Book Depot: http://www.bookdepot.com
(8) Bookfinder: http://www.bookfinder.com
(9) France Antique: http://www.franceantiq.fr
(10) Half.com: http://www.half.com
(11) Powell's Books: http://www.powells.com
(12) Rhinosales.com: http://www.rhinosales.com
(13) UKBookWorld: http://UKBookWorld.com

c) Motion Pictures
(1) Distribution Video: http://www.dva.com
(2) Video Oyster: http://www.VideoOyster.com

d) Sound Recordings
(1) A-1 Record Finders: http://www.aonerecordfinders.com
(2) Berkshire Record Outlet: http://www.broinc.com
(3) CDChoice: http://cdchoice.com
(4) CD Trackdown: http://www.cdtrackdown.com
(5) GEMM: http://www.gemm.com
(6) Hancock and Monks: http://www.hancockandmonks.co.uk
(7) Harold Moores Records: http://www.haroldmoores.com/index.html
(8) Loran Records: http://www.loranrecords.com
(9) Nauck's Vintage Records: http://www.78rpm.com
(10) Norbeck, Peters, and Ford: http://www.norpete.com
(11) Parnassus Records: http://www.parnassusrecords.com
(12) Recordfinders.com: http://www.recordfinders.com
(13) Yankee Music Search: http://www.yankeemusic.com

e) Serials
(1) Alfred Jaeger, Inc.: http://www.ajaeger.com
(2) Schmidt Periodicals GmbH & Periodicals Service Company: http://www.backsets.com

Glossary of Out-of-Print Book Terms and Abbreviations

4to, 8vo, 12mo, etc.   Refers to the size of the book. This is based on the number of pages into which a single printed sheet has been folded to create the leaves that form the pages of a book. The fewer the folds, the larger the book. Most hardbound books are 8vo (octavo—six by nine inches, about the size of an average hardcover). To make an octavo book a printed sheet would be folded eight times to form eight leaves. A leaf contains two printed pages, one on each side. A 4to is a quarto (nine by twelve inches). A 12mo is a duodecimo (five by eight inches, about the size of an average paperback).

aeg   All edges gilt.

as new   *See* condition.

bdg   Binding.

bds   Boards; the stiff front and back parts of hardcover books.

BOMC   Book-of-the-month club.

Brodart   Plastic cover which is used to protect a book's dust jacket.

bumped   Dented; usually occurs on a book's edges and corners due to use.

chipped   Small tears, or small pieces missing from the edges of pages or dust jacket.

cocked   The spine is twisted so that the boards will not line up evenly with each other.

condition   The following are standard bookseller terms generally used to described the following conditions of a book. Abbreviations for these terms are: "near fine"—NF; "good"—G; "fine"—F; "very good"—VG; "poor"—P; "fair" and "as new" have no abbreviation. When two abbreviations or terms of condition are used together with a slash, the first term generally refers to the condition of the book and the second term to the condition of the dust jacket, for example, VG/VG means that the book is in very good condition and the dust jacket is also in very good condition. Term definitions below are quoted from the *AB Bookman's Weekly*.

As new: To be used only when a book is in the same immaculate condition as that in which it was published. There can be no defects, no missing pages, no library stamps, etc., and the dustjacket (if it was issued with one) must be perfect, without any tears.

Fine: Approaches the "as new" condition, but without being crisp. For the use of the term "fine" there must also be no defects, etc., and if the jacket has a small tear, or other defect, or looks worn, this should be noted.

Very good: Showing some small signs of wear—but no tears—on either binding or paper. Any defects must be noted.

Good: The average condition of a used book—worn, all pages or leaves present. Any defects must be noted.

Fair: Worn, with complete text pages (including those with maps or plates) but possibly lacking endpapers, half-title, etc. (which must be noted). Binding, jacket (if any), etc., may also be worn. All defects must be noted.

Poor: Sufficiently worn that its only merit is as a reading copy. Its text is complete and legible, but it may be soiled, scuffed, stained, or spotted and may have loose joints, hinges, pages, etc. Any missing maps or plates should still be noted.

dust jacket (DJ)   Also called dust wrapper; the paper cover, usually illustrated, placed around a book to protect its binding.

dust wrapper (DW)   *See* dust jacket.

ep   Endpapers; sheets of papers pasted onto the inside covers joining the text block to the cover. One side is pasted down onto the cover the other is left free.

exlib or ex-lib   A book that has been purchased from a library and will therefore have library stamp marks, pockets, due date slips, etc.

fair   *See* condition.

ffep   Front free endpaper; the blank sheet that is not pasted down onto the cover.

fine   *See* condition.

first edition   The first printing of the first edition; the first time a book has appeared.

foxed   Brownish spotting of paper usually due to acid content.

good   *See* condition.

half leather   A book cover in which the spine and corners are bound in leather, while the rest of the cover is in cloth or paper.

hinge   The joint (either outer or inner) of the binding of a book (the part that bends when the book is opened).

ill.   Illustrated or illustrations.

insc.   Inscribed.

laid in   A piece of paper, leaf, letter, etc. inserted but not glued into a book.

ltd.   Limited edition.

ms or mss   Manuscript.

nd   No date.

near fine   *See* condition.

pb or pbk   Paperback.

pc or price clipped   The price has been cut out, usually a small triangle from the inside dust jacket containing the price information.

poor   *See* condition.

pub.   Publisher or published.

rubbed   Indicates that the outer layer of the binding material has been rubbed off.

shaken   Book is no longer firm and crisp; textblock feels loose in the hinges.

signed   Inscribed with the author's signature.

slipcase   A container (usually cardboard) specially made to hold a book.

spine   The bound outer edge of a book.

teg   Top edge gilt.

tipped in   A sheet or sheets added after the book was produced through the use of minute amounts of glue along the edges of the sheet(s) to be inserted.

tp   Title page.

uncut   Describes older books whose page edges were not trimmed.

very good   *See* condition.

vol.   Volume.

Bibliography

Ahearn, Allen, and Patricia Ahearn. *Book Collecting: A Comprehensive Guide.* New York: Putnam Publishing, 1995.

Ahearn, Allen, and Patricia Ahearn. *Book Collecting 2000: A Comprehensive Guide.* New York: Putnam's Sons, 2000.

Ahearn, Allen, and Patricia Ahearn. *Collected Books: The Guide to Values 1998.* New York: Putnam Publishing, 1997.

Antiquarian Booksellers Association of American. *Membership Directory.* Serial. Published annually.

Bickers, Patrick M. "New Ways to Acquire Old Books." *College & Research Libraries News* (March 2002): 173–75.

Black, Diane. "In Search of Out-of-Print Books: The Past, the Present and the Future." *Georgia Library Quarterly* 35, no. 1 (spring 1998): 11–17.

Carter, John. *ABC for Book Collectors.* 7th ed. Edited by Nicolas Barker. New Castle, Del.: Oak Knoll Press, 1995.

Childress, Boyd, and Barbara Nelson. "Out-of-Print Acquisitions: A Dual Perspective." *The Southeastern Librarian* 37 (winter 1987): 121–24.

Craddock, Jim. *VideoHound's Golden Movie Retriever 2002.* Detroit, Mich.: Gale Group, 2001.

Drake, "Finding Out-of-Print Titles on the Internet," *Texas Library Journal* 73, no. 2 (summer 1997): 86–87.

Ellis, Ian C. *Book Finds: How to Find, Buy, and Sell Used and Rare Books.* New York: Berkley Publishing Group, 2001.

Ethridge, James M., and Karen Ethridge, eds. *Antiquarian, Specialty, and Used Book Sellers: A Subject Guide and Directory, 1997–98.* 2nd ed. Detroit, Mich.: Omnigraphics, 1997.

Flinchbaugh, Melissa. "Biz of Acq—Out-of-Print Books: A Practical, Web-based Solution." *Against the Grain* 13, no. 1 (2001): 20–23.

Geller, Marilyn. "Trading Places: Back Issues Find a Home on the Net." *Serials Review* 23, no. 1 (spring 1997): 47–57.

Kachmar, Diane. "Resources for Foreign Out-of-Print Books: A New World Order." *Library Collections Acquisitions and Technical Services* 24, no. 2 (2000): 327.

Landesman, Margaret. "Out-of-Print and Secondhand Markets," in *Understanding the Business of Library Acquisitions*, edited by Karen A. Schmidt. Chicago: American Library Association, 1990. 187–205.

Maltin, Leonard. *Leonard Maltin's 2002 Movie & Video Guide*. New York: Plume, 2001.

Robinson, Ruth E. *Buy Books Where—Sell Books Where, 1994–1995*. 9th ed. Morgantown, W.Va.: Ruth E. Robinson Books, 1994.

R.R. Bowker Company. *Bowker's Complete Video Directory 2002*. New Providence, N.J.: R.R. Bowker, 2001.

Tafuri, Narda. "Biz of Acq—The Out of Print Marketplace." *Against the Grain* 10, no. 1 (February 1998): 68–70.